Praise For
Get Out Of Your Head And Onto Your Purpose

"What a Right On Time Book for the business minded! -

Demario and Dawn have done it Again with their Innovation and ability to pull greatness " Out of our head". I simply cannot say enough about this Book and the magic it will create for those holding back their own success. Thank you both for getting inside our heads to make our Dreams a Reality. Signed your Very Pleased Customer."

-Tinisha L. Springs, Owner of TLS & ASSOCIATES

"DeMario and Dawn Nicole's teachings, strategies & branding solutions are nationally renowned and used in many of our colleges today. I'm excited to read all that they produce, and highly recommend [to] all to read their books and tune into their keynote talks."

-Darryl G. Irving, Owner of Classy Pool & Spa Services

"We are excited to read and learn! It came at a time when we needed a little nudge. Much success!"

-Mr. & Mrs. Poole

"I decided to pre-order the book after speaking with authors DeMario and Dawn Nicole McIlwain. I like their positive, upbeat approach to action planning. I've accomplished a lot of what I wanted to do. But there is much more in the world to explore and a lot more that can be done. Devoted to lifelong learning, I'm always studying, researching and looking for fresh ideas to help jump start my next venture, activity or strategy. I think I'll find some tips in....Onto Your Purpose."

-Mark Irving., Real Estate Investor

"I've had a vision and a dream inside of me for so long, but my over-thinking and self-doubts have been keeping them hostage, that I know.... I need help. This book spoke to me immediately!"

-Altrea M., Licensed Insurance Agent

"I had the opportunity to meet Dawn when she was exit[ing] corporate America onto starting her business and marrying the love of her life, DeMario! "Talking about getting out of your head onto your purpose" they've done just that! And I have been blessed to see it and receive it! I hope you find this book as motivating as the couple that wrote it!"

-LaDonna Wright, The Relationship Nurse

"I am a Certified Leadership Coach and Motivational speaker and even when you are in the business of inspiring and motivating others, you often times need encouragement yourself that you are on the right track and to keep pressing forward. So, I am super excited about getting my copy of, Get Out of Your Head and Onto Your Purpose, in an effort to motivate and encourage me on my own personal journey."

-G. Patrick Griffin, Author, Certified Leadership Coach and Motivational Speaker

---

"Wow, I am so excited for the book, Onto Your Purpose, to be released! Personally, having had the privilege to work with Dawn as she mentored me when I transitioned out of the military was amazing! With the book on the horizon, the more people who can receive DeMario & Dawn's heart & passion for Servant Leadership. I'm looking forward to having nuggets and tips at my fingertips to reference at a moment's notice."

-Oneika Brown, Executive Administrative Assistant

"I was inspired by the knowledge and passion you have to empower others! Thank You"

-Dean Harris

"This book is right on time! We are encouraged AND inspired! Get Out Of Your Head & Onto Your Purpose. We definitely will!"

-Monique and Rayford Byrd

"I'm excited to receive my book. Dawn's energy and enthusiasm has been a great help to me to get some projects started. I'm sure the wisdom from this duo will help me make it to the finish line!"

-Margo Scurry

"A Business Trailblazer-

Mrs. Dawn Nicole McIlwain & I spoke at a mutual friend's inaugural conference in 2018; she was beyond fired up and engaging. She left us so many resources, hope & free access to her multimillion dollar success tool. We immediately connected. I know this book is a jewel for everyone ready to begin and or expand. Elated we reside within the same city. Get yours and a few as gifts."

-Shonda S. Caines, Wellness Catalyst & Vegan Fitness Chef

"I am excited about this book because [DeMario & Dawn Nicole] are such a phenomenal couple and the book is a "Must Have" for me!"

-Peggy Frazier

"Wishing DeMario and Dawn Much continued success in life and business. I am thankful to be counted among their associates. Proverbs 4:6-7"

-John Cash, Narmer Group LLC

Real Stories. Real Steps. Real Solutions

Get Out of Your Head and Onto Your Purpose.
When THINKING stops & DOING starts

by Demario and Dawn Nicole McIlwain

BrandDisco© Publishing D/B/A BrandDisco© LLC

BRANDDISCO LLC
3160 HWY 160 STE 103
Fort Mill, S.C. 29715
(704) 709-0329 ext. 101

Copyright © 2019 by DeMario and Dawn Nicole McIlwain

All Rights Reserved. This book may not be reproduced in whole or in part, stored in a retrieval system, or transmitted in any form or by any means electronic, mechanical, or other without written permission from the publisher, except by a reviewer, who may quote brief passages in review and assigns its rightful credits thereof.

Cover design: DeMario & Dawn Nicole McIlwain
Interior design: DeMario McIlwain
Typography: DeMario & Dawn Nicole McIlwain

Originally published in The United States by BrandDisco© Publishing D/B/A BrandDisco© LLC 2019

Table of Contents:

Introduction - Overview & Summary 13

<u>Chapter 1:</u>
TRUST -Taking Risks Under Suppose Threat 17

<u>Chapter 2:</u>
FEAR -Failure of Each Action & Result 27

<u>Chapter 3:</u>
PERFECT -Perceived Expectations Restricting Forward, Execution, Completion & Tasks 39

<u>Chapter 4:</u>
DOUBT -Debating Over Uncertainties Before Trying 45

<u>Chapter 5:</u>
TRUTH -Time Reveals Unique Talents & Habits 51

<u>Chapter 6:</u>
TIME -The Initial Mental Entrapment 61

<u>Chapter 7:</u>
MOTIVATION -Making Opportunity The Immediate Vision And Top Initiative Over Necessities *DeMario's Story* 69

<u>Chapter 8:</u>
DRIVE -Determined Resilient Inspiration & Valor for Excellence *Dawn Nicole's Story* 79

<u>Chapter 9:</u>
LEVERAGE - Learning Every Valuable & Eligible Resource Available for Greater Expansion 87

<u>Chapter 10:</u>
Success Stories from Everyday People 97

Table of Contents:

Chapter 11:
Twenty-Nine Winning Tips with Actionable Strategies & Simple Exercises for Getting Out of Your Head 109
About The Authors:
About DeMario & Dawn Nicole McIlwain 123
Acknowledgements
Special Thanks 127

Introduction

Chances are, you picked up this book because you, or someone you know, has a real desire to achieve more success yet might be re-thinking, re-tweaking or trying to perfect every experience out of the gate; which is usually counter-productive to any progress.

You may even feel frustrated, disappointed or discouraged about not having accomplished all that you set forth to do in your life or career.

Despite this, we want to applaud you for taking the first step in owning your own success by purchasing this book.

Through this book of Real Stories, Real Steps & Real Solutions, you will find the strategies you need to get out of your head and onto your purpose by adopting the art of mindless thinking.

When THINKING stops and DOING starts.

As a Husband and Wife Team, who spends a great deal of time helping others transform their invisible values into high impact success, we became transfixed with mastering mindless thinking concepts, after seeing our own visions & goals skyrocket once we got rid of those self-imposed complexities.

Yes, you read that right, "self-imposed complexities."

These are the complexities we bring upon ourselves through our own self-imposed fears, doubts or uncertainties leading to overthinking and under-performing.

Right now, you might be wondering what kind of person would desire to have more out of life yet would intentionally over-complicate their visions or goals to the point of no return.

Introduction

And how it could be possible, that the same person fighting to be successful also be the very person getting in their own way.

Better yet, you might be secretly wondering, if this describes you.

Well, let's start by being honest.

-Do you start things that you don't finish?

-Do you set unrealistic goals that are impossible to meet?

-Do you feel you cannot operate off-script?

If you said yes to any of these questions, you might be creating undue complexities stemming from hidden fears, doubts or uncertainties around your goals.

Don't be alarmed, you aren't alone and being open and honest is where it all begins.

Surprisingly, we found an entire population of people who over-complicated things that should have been relatively simple.

We discovered this was happening more often than one might suspect, which is why we were determined to bring about a solution.

Our hope is that more people adopt the mindless thinking concepts we've outlined in this book leading to more success in less time.

Introduction

Through this book, we'll teach you the mindless thinking concepts that will allow you to:

-Trust Your Gut

-Live Unscripted

-Value Quality Over Quantity.

To begin, we will introduce you to a number of reasons some struggle to get out of their heads and strategies for getting onto your purpose.

Chapter 1:
TRUST
(Taking Risks Under Suppose Threat)

"Don't judge each day by the harvest you reap but by the seeds that you plant".
-Robert Louis Stevenson

Chapter 1: TRUST

By definition, improvisation means the art, or act of improvising, composing, uttering, executing, or arranging something without previous preparation.

No script, rehearsal or practice necessary.

While that might seem simple, or easy enough, it is arguably one of the hardest challenges and fears faced by many.

In fact, think back to a time when you asked someone to introduce you or bring you up to speak at a show or an event.

Chances are, no matter how well they know you, they might have asked you to provide them with an intro-script for them to read as they brought you up.

Depending on your relationship to them, you might have found yourself thinking… *"You know me pretty well, just introduce me as you normally would."*

However, they most likely preferred and appreciated a script as a point of reference.

If this was the case, they are like many people.

Regardless of how well we might know each other, or how familiar we might be in our respective areas of expertise, many don't trust their inner instincts to guide them through an entire experience.

This is because we are afraid to be led by our feelings.

Despite our Grandmother's best advice of trusting our gut, society has taught us not to trust our emotions and feelings

Chapter 1: TRUST

and rather stick with the things we can see and touch instead.
But why? What do we fear could happen?

What will we say, or not say, or do, or not do, that would be completely detrimental to our cause?

And what if the answer was nothing.

Absolutely no impact at all, because you'd achieve the same outcome.

Meaning, the script was nothing more than a pointless, meaningless, placebo, only set in place to offer you a false sense of security.

Cliff notes of the book you authored.

A picture of the painting you drew.

A knock-off of the song you composed.

What if the same script designed to keep you on track and hinged to your objective, had really been your hindrance the entire time?

Ponder this. Have you ever met someone who spent a great deal of time and money getting prepared for a major event and when it was all said and done, they didn't need half the things they'd prepared for?

This is because what many people don't realize is, the thing that people want most from us, lies deep within us.

It can't be bought, taught or duplicated and surprisingly, it's the thing we work so hard to hide the most.

Chapter 1: TRUST

This thing is called **'our authentic self.'**

Who we are to the core.

What we know in our spirit.

The collection of values we possess naturally.

Our authentic self is genuine, holds undisputed origin and is the first founding member of our being.

It doesn't need bells, whistles, and flares, nor a wingman or wing-woman to usher it in.

The authentic self can outwit, outsmart and outlast, the manufactured self any day.

Despite this, many won't let it have its own stage because we don't trust our authentic selves to behave, be compelling and quite frankly, be enough.

As a result, we embellish it, dress it up with fancy décor, solicit the help of colorful entourages, *(a.k.a the script)*, and bury our authentic self - deep within material layers so that it can't be exposed, heard or detected.

We pick and choose when it can come out to play, and when the authentic self, (rebellious and longing to be heard, as it may), speaks out of turn, it causes us great discourse as we critically chastise ourselves. **"Stupid! So Dumb! Ugh, I can't believe I just said that!"**

We reprimand its unpredictable behavior like that of a two-year old child, all the while creating the very delinquency, we despise by keeping our authentic selves caged - like a rabid dog.

Chapter 1: TRUST

However, if you know a thing, or two about parenting, then you know that the best way to create and develop a well-behaved child in a social setting is to expose that child to social settings more often.

Civility is a learned behavior; and like our children, if you want the authentic self to be more in sync, acclimated and an aligned representative, then you must introduce it more often.

Unhinged and Unscripted.

We must expose, embrace and engage its essence by allowing the authentic self to flow in its natural habitat by trusting that we know more than we think, and more than we show.

We must also trust that all by itself, the authentic self is enough.

No additives or preservatives required.

However, it's important to note, that after years of suppressing its nature, the road to trusting one's authentic self won't be easy.

Yet with anything, the more we practice operating off-script, giving value unrehearsed and trusting our gut instincts, the more in-tuned with the authentic self we will become.

Now chances are if you're reading this book, you are probably thinking…"easier said than done."

Chapter 1: TRUST

You might even be thinking how horribly irresponsible it sounds to show-up unprepared.

Let's address both concerns separately.

I can't operate off-script:

First, if you're like most people, you may have bought into the lie that you are no-good when operating off-script.

You probably fed yourself this un-truth for so many years now, it's likely that you actually believe it.

It's like the self-proclaimed genius kid, who tells everyone how much, he or she, sucks at English yet loves math.

This might be the farthest thing from the truth; however, the mind believes what it's been told day in and day out.

Also, just because this is what you've always allowed yourself to believe, doesn't make it the truth.

The reality is, if you've never exercised being authentic, in its truest capacity, then you don't know what you don't know.

It's unprofessional to not be prepared:

Secondly, society makes us believe that being prepared is half the battle, when in fact it's responsible for only 15% of the battle.

Trust me, we realize this news is amongst some of the most shocking you will ever read and yet it's true.

Chapter 1: TRUST

Think about it like this. How many years of schooling did we receive vs. the amount of knowledge we actually applied?

How many years of our kids' lives did we spend trying to prepare them for scenarios that actually never happened or when they did, strategic thinking, gut reaction, and reflex played a bigger role than everything prepared?

How many times did you study for a major test and almost none of the questions resembled what you studied?

In fact, there are countless military professionals who spent years preparing for battle and when they arrived, it was gut instinct that kept them alive.

It was grit that kept them sharp and quick thinking that saved the day.

This proves that the best muscle to exercise is reflex, instinct and critical thinking through impromptu reactions to what we don't know is coming.

Being over-prepared causes us to become too comfortable and doesn't allow us to respond to that for which we didn't prepare for.

Let's take stage play productions as an example.

A good director starts off a new project with providing the cast members a script allowing each actor to get acclimated to the flow of the full production. *(i.e. Characters, lines, cadence, lights, soundtrack, etc.)*

Chapter 1: TRUST

However, there must come a point where the director needs to know if the cast has committed their script to memory.

This is important for many reasons.
One of which is that an actor cannot fully embody the character with a paper in their face.

To be and feel authentic to the role, they will need to make the character their own.

However, a more important reason is that, as the production nears its opening date, the strategy changes from the actors committing the lines to memory to ensuring they understand improvisation.

What to do, or how to recover if they or their cast member forgets a line so that the show goes on seamlessly.

This component becomes just as critical, planning for the unknown by strengthening that reflex muscle.

Later in the book, we will provide some great tips you can use to work on this.

-end chapter 1-

Chapter 2:
FEAR
(Failure of Each Action & Result)

"Never confuse a single defeat with a final defeat."
-F. Scott Fitzgerald

Chapter 2: FEAR

Some business owner's first steps into entrepreneurship are based on pure passion.

The love they have for their craft or talents they possess.

They see their products or gifts as valuable, although very few may have a business concept to prove its marketability.

Yet still, without a doubt, they might begin producing the results and learning the best business practices along the way.

On the other hand, many have great skills and talents within a certain field yet find themselves stuck inside their minds carefully trying to find the balance between working for someone and owning a business.

Or, stuck working at a place that does not align with what they love to do.

Let's take John for example… A master at wood carvings and furniture design.

John spent many days after work in his garage carving out unique furniture designs from wood.

He admired his many collections as they hung around the walls, each piece telling a story of a place and time.

During the day, John worked as a delivery driver who delivered beverages to the local shopping markets.

Although the pay was decent and the work hours weren't demanding, John often found himself counting down the minutes in the day to hurry back home & finish the designs he had started.

Chapter 2: FEAR

As time went on, many other people started to hear about John's collections and would ask if they could come by his garage to view the designs.

On occasion, John would give a tour explaining each piece in detail.

He could talk on and on about the designs, the style of wood and the inspiration behind it.

Quite often, many of John's pieces would be purchased for thousands of dollars but when asked why this wasn't his full-time business, John would quickly reply with many excuses as to why he couldn't leave his job.

Like, how he had researched the furniture market and how it was declining.

Or how his weekly pay gave him the funds he needed for his supplies and equipment.

John would also receive job offers from design teams from other furniture companies, which he had no interest in, due to thinking he already had the best job for his lifestyle.

Soon, John received a big promotion at his job which demanded more hours but at higher pay.

He found himself spending less and less time in his garage creating due to late evening work at the job, which he hated.

Although he still had a passion for his creations, he often found himself too tired to create, and simply sold pieces from time to time.

Without his added talent, the collection was soon gone.

Chapter 2: FEAR

One year as John was filing his taxes, he couldn't help but notice how much money he made selling pieces of his collection versus the money made from his job.

He wondered how he had not noticed this before.

He couldn't understand why he never took his passion serious enough to start his own business, nor the cause of his fear of leaving his job.

John was the perfect example of someone who spent too much time thinking of the 'WHY NOTS' while never accepting the reality that his passion & talents could be his purpose to a successful career.

This type of mentality could be caused by Cherophobia – A mental fear of being happy and afraid to make that first step towards living your best life.

One of the symptoms most related to Cherophobia is... "passing on an opportunity that could lead to positive life changes due to the fear that something bad will happen."

So, let's break it down.

What are the top 5 things that could have happened to John if he had simply followed his purpose?

> 1. John may have had to quit his current position or role to find one that aligns with his passion.

> 2. John may have had to take a brief pay cut while he continued to build on his skills and launch his new business.

3. John's friends and or family might think he's plain crazy and not support his transition.

4. John could experience the feeling of loss and need help from others to make sure he reaches his goals.

5. John may find out, although passionate about his talents, he lacked the ability to run a business and would need to hire and trust others to handle his day to day operations.

The point is, John would have at least tried.

Another question you may ask yourself is, did John set an impossible goal or standard?

We all know the person who's waiting for the perfect time to do that one thing they talk about every time you see them.

They might even say…" When I save "X" amount of money, I'm leaving that job to start my own business, or when I hit "X" amount of years, I'm only going to do what I love."

We call this person The Serial Perfectionist.

The one who always has to have everything laid out, just-right, before they can take their first step.

However, the problem is, as soon as they get to the edge, something else happens adding a new goal or standard that must be met prior to them moving toward their passion.

Self-imposed layering. Adding-on layers of perfect standards.

Although this could be John's problem, we're going to assume it's not yours, *right?*

Chapter 2: FEAR

Now let's imagine your life being picture-perfect.

Everyone compliments you on your position, possessions and your model-family.

(They forget to ask about your happiness...but that's okay.)

You have mentally decided this is what the good life looks like.

Although these might not be things that give you butterflies, you look good and that's all that matters. Right?

Who needs to be happy living their best life, or doing the things they love most?

And if you think you're living your best life now, or that finding your true passion is a mystery, answering these questions will help.

- Do you love what you currently do?
- Do you think & talk about it all the time?
- Do you get self-satisfaction from it?
- Would you do it for free if all of your needs were met?

All important questions when you start questioning whether or not you're living your purpose filled life.

Here's another perspective of how you should be thinking about your passion.

Today you do _"X"_ for a living and you make _"X"_ per year doing it.
On average you spend _"X"_ hours per week on it and it took you _"X"_ years to get to this level.
It took you _"X"_ years to get to this level.

Also, let's add-in the studying you've done.

Maybe college-level or business courses, trial and error, building relationships or just your sheer drive that got you here.

Either way, you've worked hard therefore what's the difference?

If you spent as many hours per week x's the same amount of years perfecting and building your passion and purpose, you would actually make much more than _____ "X" ____ a year.

Now if you discovered through this brief exercise, you are not currently living in your passion & higher purpose, below are a few great points to focus on.

With this said, if you've been neglecting your true passion and purpose, maybe it's time to advance to the next level.

You've mastered the art, now you can teach or train others to do the same thing.

F.E.A.R of Criticism:

Let's discuss the fear of criticism, that fear that makes well-deserving people feel intimidated about releasing or showcasing anything less than perfect, for fear of less than favorable reviews.

Chapter 2: FEAR

Let's look at a more common example of an everyday working woman, we'll call Linda.

Linda had a booming six-figure business helping other business owners and non-profits research and write grants.

She was well-liked and amazing at the work she delivered.

One day, I asked her why she never included speaking or workshops as a part of her offerings.

I remember she looked at me squarely in the eyes and replied with… "I'd never put myself out there to be judged, open for public scrutiny or picked apart by others in my field."

I was dumbfounded and taken back by this response.

I couldn't believe someone that I truly looked up to, admired and saw as high successful, might have been secretly afraid to be vulnerable or challenged by others and it was this fear alone that was stopping her from being greater.

Was Linda afraid that others might find a flaw, a typo, an inconsistency?

And then what?

What would happen as a result of this find?

Would it be a career-ending blow?

The beginning of doomsday?

Chapter 2: FEAR

An apocalyptic event of biblical portion?

Of course, you're sensing a hint of sarcasm because, in actuality, none of these things would happen.

Instead, allow us to put this into perspective for you.

- Reporters mis-speak and recant their stories.
- Columnists and Bloggers have an editorial oversight and simply update their stories.
- CEOs of companies tweet something insensitive on social media and issue an apology.
- Authors are made aware of grammatical errors and issue a revision.
- Car manufacturers have a faulty part and issue a recall.
- Drug companies learn about an unforeseen side-effect and pull the product from store shelves.
- Apple adds new features to the iPhone and issue a version update almost monthly.

The point?

None of these public figures, influencers or big box brands have a fear of showing up imperfectly.

They just show up.

What each of these examples have in common is progress, which is the enemy of perfection.

Fear or not, being perfect hasn't stopped the original product, service or concept from getting out there.

Chapter 2: FEAR

This is because the reward is greater than the risk.

The point is life happens knee-deep in imperfections and yet, it still goes on.

We are fully aware that for many, this notion is much easier said than done.

Especially if you come from an environment where you are penalized for your mistakes.

After all, it can be seen as a struggle to walk that fine line of not wanting to be a perfectionist, while also, not wanting to be careless.

"So, what's the happy medium between the two?" You might ask.

For starters, there are some key things to remember when it comes to striking a balance between not being perfect yet being intentional.

Look at the appropriation of what's being delivered.

Are we talking heart surgery, where extreme diligence, precision, and acute focus are required?

Or are we talking a presentation where thirty people are coming to hear you discuss a topic, you're already an expert at?

Consider the level of criticality.

It's not about being perfect, it's about being intentional with your thoughts, beliefs and purpose.

Chapter 2: FEAR

Ultimately, as we push past our FEAR, (Failure of Each Action & Result) let's be reminded that done is better than perfect.

-end chapter 2-

Chapter 3:
PERFECT
(Perceived Expectations Restricting Forward, Execution, Completion & Tasks)

"We have to do the best we are capable of.
This is our sacred human responsibility."
-Albert Einstein

Chapter 3: PERFECT

Did you know that perfectionism can be a curse that paralyzes productivity?

It's true.

Although many of us are raised to believe that there's no such thing as perfect, some people still continue to get stuck in the frothy pursuit of perfectionism causing delays and procrastination that kills opportunities.

Despite this fact, one can't help but wonder where this unrelenting, unyielding & unforgiving desire to be perfect comes from.

Especially during a time where the world is craving authenticity, vulnerability and an utter sense of real experiences.

In fact, perfectionism is one of the most despised traits among co-working groups, and the reason Reality T.V. is at an all-time high due to its anti-perfection nature.

You see, we as a society have spoken.

We don't want flawless, impeccable and cookie-cutter versions of life. Instead, we want real, raw, human emotions, relatability & vulnerability.

Despite this, many won't dare to show up or take an action unless every "I" is dotted, and every "T" is crossed.

One famous example of perfectionism at its best, is the story of Jazz Saxophonist Great, John Coltrane.

Yes, you read that name correctly, John Coltrane.

Chapter 3: PERFECT

It's been reported through recent documentaries that Coltrane's perfectionism may have led to a tumultuous backlash among some of his most loyal and faithful fans, when he began adopting more experiential musical-styles in his later years.

We understand if this news comes as a shock to some of Coltrane's younger-generation fans, who often regard him as being one of Jazz's Greats producing some of the biggest jazz albums of all time. *(i.e. A Love Supreme, My Favorite Things, etc.)*

While these critical acclaims are certainly well-deserved, it's been reported that some of Coltrane's hidden musical collections have an interesting history of perfectionism.

Coming off the popularity of previous classics like, "A Love Supreme" and "My Favorite Things," Coltrane felt compelled to perfect and further his musical powers beyond what he'd done.

Armed with a perfectionist mindset and need to out-do himself, Coltrane produced two follow-up albums entitled, "Ascension" and "Meditations."

Both were wildly more abstract than his previous works, and both designed to appeal to his fans who had *"more acquired"* musical taste for complex melodic rhythms.

Coltrane's unrelenting drive to release his greatest work of all time, led to him spending weeks locked away in an upstairs room of his family's home.

This happened to coincide with the arrival of the couple's newborn son and with him spending long hours composing

Chapter 3: PERFECT

and writing, his wife was only instructed to interrupt him for meals or other necessities.

This would go on for several months, as Coltrane became increasingly more insistent on introducing his fans to a newer, deeper & experiential musical sound better than before.

His album would eventually release causing Coltrane to conduct live performances of his new compilations at various music events.

However, to his dismay, many fans ended up extremely disappointed finding his new music to be too overtly abstract and far more inferior than his past classics.

Some fans even went as far as to leave the show in the middle of his set stating how they had wasted their time and money.

We can only imagine the disappointment Coltrane may have felt as some of his fans insinuated - that he might have been BETTER before he tried to be his BEST.

We found this part of Coltrane's story to be utterly intriguing from a more human perspective since it deeply related to the perfectionist that has the potential to lurk inside of us all.

The irony here is that it would seem the more Coltrane wanted to reach higher heights for his fans, the more his fans longed for him to remain grounded and steadfast into the styles that had once "won over" their hearts.

You'll notice we've placed special emphasis on the word. "Won."
This is because some of us keep trying to win, not realizing we've already won, as in what seemed to be the case with Coltrane.

Chapter 3: PERFECT

Perfectionism comes in all forms and doesn't care who it strikes or impacts.

Coltrane's reported story was just one example of this.

Many described him as being on a never-ending quest to perfect his musical talents, however, the harder he tried, the more he pushed away those he wanted to connect with most.

As is the case with many people who suffer from perfectionism.

Despite this, we are of the opinion that Coltrane was, and will always be, one of Jazz's Late Greats!

Remember, there is no such thing as perfect. The world is awaiting your gifts and your gifts will make room for you, as they are.

-end chapter 3-

Chapter 4:
DOUBT
(Debating Over Uncertainties Before Trying)

"The scariest moment is always just before you start."
-Stephen King

Chapter 4: DOUBT

We've all heard of writing down the pros & cons before making any major decision.

This practice began in the 16th century and is simply an abbreviation of the Latin phrase *pro et contra*, meaning "for and against."

It was first used by Benjamin Franklin in 1772 as he advised his friend and fellow scientist Joseph Priestley to divide a sheet of paper in half creating two columns.

One for pros and the other for cons, when it came to making a difficult decision.

Since its early origin, this practice has been used by many and is still held in high regard, as a great problem-solving tool. However, if the question is whether or not to follow your passion or purpose, is that really a fair debate in need of a sound decision, or is that simply a form of self-doubt to begin with?

Determining your reasons for "why" and "why not" can be challenging when it comes to going forward with that thing, that one thing that you are constantly thinking about.

You feel a strong urge to just go forward but then comes the doubt of how to make it happen or should you even make it happen in the first place.

There are too many voices in your head telling you different stories and predicting unknown outcomes, to the point that it begins to not make sense in either direction, so you find yourself just sitting still. (Procrastination.)

Chapter 4: DOUBT

Sure, there are tons of reasons we can give as to why we can't do anything, yet unless we have tried with a full effort and realistic goals, we can never simply doubt the success of anything.

A greatly relatable story would be of the unschooled, Leonardo Da Vinci who's considered one of the most famous artists in the world. He's mostly known for his painting of "Mona Lisa" and "The Last Supper."

However, what many people might not know about Da Vinci is that he suffered from self-doubt, procrastination and esteem issues.

He was also known to abandon and never finish-up projects. Da Vinci, who was employed as an engineer and inventor also conceptually invented the parachute, an improved version of the helicopter, an armored fighting vehicle, the use of solar power, the calculator and so much more.

Today, his most famous drawing linked his love for art and science called the Vitruvian Man which combines a careful reading of the ancient text with his own observation of actual human bodies.

Da Vinci is only one of many people whose talents amazed many but to him, the struggle in his mind was more damaging than the successes and accomplishments known by many.

"Believe it can be done. When you believe something can be done, really believe, your mind will find the ways to do it. Believing a solution paves the way to solution." – David J. Schwartz

Chapter 4: DOUBT

When you take a look back into your past, how many times did you abandon a great idea simply because you (or someone around you) began to doubt its outcome?

When being truthful with yourself, it makes you feel some type of way, doesn't it?

If you're like us, we have spent a lot of time watching shows like NBC's Shark Tank then kicking ourselves when simple ideas, created by people like us, turn into multi-million-dollar businesses in a few years.

We all have the ability to become greater tomorrow than we are today.

It takes pure bravery to step out of what's already known, into the darkness of what's yet to be discovered.

By asking yourself, "Am I happy here" you'll begin to open your mindset into searching for a change and going for what you REALLY want to do in life.

These traits of doubt and procrastination are self-inflicted.

We were not born with it but, somewhere in life, we picked up a few bad habits that stop our ability to dream and achieve.

When you're the creator, you create the rules and determine the outcome through pushing forward against the odds.

There is no reason to doubt your own mind and truly under no circumstances should you allow someone else to place doubt upon you, your dreams, or your passion.

-end chapter 4-

Chapter 5:
TRUTH
(Time Reveals Unique Talents & Habits)

"From error to error one discovers the entire truth."
-Sigmund Freud

Chapter 5: TRUTH

The reason we cling to the rags-to-riches stories of innovators and the behind-the-scenes success stories of business moguls is because deep down inside, we too, want to be the story others can gain inspiration from.

This nagging narrative causes us to spend our days & nights wondering and deciphering through our thoughts, what life might look like when we've reached a certain level of success for ourselves.

No matter how much we daydream about our own vision of success while nominally celebrating the wins of others, there are good things we know about ourselves for sure, despite them feeling temporarily out of reach.

For example, when it comes to 'that thing' we absolutely love, we know without a doubt, that even the smartest, most talented person in the room couldn't outdo us - even on our worst day.

It's that driving force that gives us our glimmers of hope nudging at us each day and keeping us up at night begging to be acknowledged & for us to take action.
-That's when there's nothing else to think about.

-There is no one else to ask the question.

 -And certainly, no more time to waste.

It's time for our truths, our passions & our purposes to manifest.
And no one can do it but you.

You are the only one that can get you out of your head and onto your purpose. If you're still reading this book, then it's likely you are ready to do exactly that.

Chapter 5: TRUTH

Let's take a look at Debbi...

Debbi lived as a happy housewife supporting the efforts of her husband as he was trying to start an investment firm.

As simple as it seems, one night at a dinner party she was asked by her husband's future client *"what do you do?"*

This conversation led to an embarrassing moment for Debbi as she didn't have an impressive response to match the caliber of the people in the room, which left her husband's future client puzzled.

From there, Debbi wanted to be somebody more.

Her truth was, she simply wasn't happy being a 20-yr. old housewife.

Having held a job since the tender age of 13, she was accustomed to hard work ethic.

After the dinner party, Debbi continued to spend days wondering how to become more like the vision she saw in her head.

Remembering the words her father once told her...
"wealth was doing what you loved," she realized she had a great love for baking cookies. Something she had been doing since her early childhood.

Although Debbi was young in age, and had little money or past experience, she was eventually able to turn her love for baking her cookies into a business through her, *"never give up"* mentality.

Chapter 5: TRUTH

Through the years, starting from 1977 and beyond, Debbi's little cookie business grew into over 650 retail bakeries in the United States and over 80 in 11 different countries and is currently a $450 Million Dollar company called Mrs. Fields.

You have to ask yourself; do you think once Debbi admitted her truth of not wanting to settle as a housewife, this is what caused her to evolve into a multi-million dollar business owner?

Well, some would say the truth shall set you free and your "Gifts" will always make room for you.

The point is, when you take any action toward building upon your purpose, you have to admit to what you will no longer settle for.

You must admit that where you are today is not where you desire to be tomorrow.

It's just that simple.

When you're sick and tired of being sick and tired, you will allow your mind to open up and explore new opportunities, dreams and things that bring upon a grand purpose into your life and how you want to live it.

This may not come easy, but the results are well worth it.

Succumbing to your truth is a means of understanding the differences between your passion, purpose and hope.

We all have dreams of becoming "X" and some will argue that those dreams are based on passion or even purpose.

Chapter 5: TRUTH

Let's break it down further...

To get a clearer understanding of the difference, we have to tell the story of a man we'll call Tim.

Tim loved to sing every moment he got and was not shy about telling anyone how singing was his true passion.

He found it hard to keep a steady job, especially if it interfered with his music.

Month after month, Tim spent most of his time and money in recording studios producing different songs he wrote.

With every paycheck he earned, or borrowed funds, he would invest it into his music career.

Many times, this left Tim without money to pay his bills or able to afford the cost of his own apartment, but family and friends supported him as much as they could.

He was always welcome to sleep on a couch, here are there, as well as get in a few good home-cooked meals from friends and loved ones.

It became public knowledge that you could find Tim at any and every open mic and karaoke spot in town showcasing his talent.

Tim believed in his passion and made it his purpose in life to become the next top R&B singer and win many Grammy awards from his songs and in his words, he was going to pay back everyone who helped him along the way.

Chapter 5: TRUTH

As we stated, Tim invested many hours and thousands of dollars into his music career over a series of years. Although Tim worked feverishly throughout the years on his indie music career distributing his own CD's, he never really sold much and they often ended-up stacked somewhere in a closet.

Despite this, Tim always believed in himself simply brushing-off his disappointing sales while promising that his next album was going to be the next big one!

He also auditioned for all of the top talent shows (i.e. America's Got Talent, American Idol, The X Factor, The Voice, etc.) yet never made it on to the 2nd round.

Although things didn't look good, Tim knew his time was coming and all he had to do was keep-on pushing, keep-on working and you probably guessed it... *"Keep hope alive!"*

(I think we've all known a Tim or have been in Tim's shoes.)

Let's get back to Tim.

Time would pass and Tim began to notice all of the new singers who'd started gracing the major stages year after year and none of them was him.

As this humbling reality begin to overtake him, he started to seek out answers as to why he wasn't getting his "big break" in the music business.

As in anything, when you seek the truth, it will come to you.

Chapter 5: TRUTH

After inquiring and many requests for candid feedback, Tim was forced to face the awful truth from record executives of whom he trusted for sound advice and opinions.

The following counsel was given to him, *"Tim, although your passion is great and your drive for success is amazing, your voice is not that great and at your age of 55, the market isn't open to your abstract lyrics, sound or appearance."*

The record company executive went on to state, although this might not be the news Tim was hoping to hear, he felt Tim would be a great talent manager for their company because of his passion for music. He also added that Tim's dedication to completing projects would really help someone else get to the next level and asked if he'd be open for the job.

Tim being very disappointed, declined the position and last we heard, was still hanging around the open mics showcasing his music and waiting on his next big break.

Although we could say this was a harsh way to crush someone's dreams, the reality is simple.

For years, the multi-million-dollar music industry has sought out young fresh talent to promote to their buying public.

Just as anything, the music industry is a business and Tim's talent didn't fit the mold.

Therefore, beyond passion or even hope, Tim missed all of the signs and never got out of his head the thought of being that super star.

Chapter 5: TRUTH

You may be asking, what signs?

-Sign number 1, after many invested hours and money, his finished products never returned the investments he put in.

-Sign number 2, after many auditions he never made it to the 2nd round of any showcase.

-Sign number 3, his relentless pursuit of his one-sided dream robbed him of living a purpose filled life.

-Sign number 4, Tim never assessed the business side of his passion and assumed he had the right tools (i.e. Voice, age, sound, etc.) they were looking for.

This serves as just another example of how some people get buried inside of their own heads and essentially miss out on their deeper purpose by being unwilling to succumb to the truth.

-end chapter 5-

Chapter 6:
TIME
(The Initial Mental Entrapment)

"The proper function of man is to live, not to exist. I shall not waste my days in trying to prolong them. I shall use my time."
-Jack London

Chapter 6: TIME

"I don't have enough time", is one of the first things we hear from people who have a desire to become something different.

This phrase is usually followed by the task they want to accomplish but have yet to start.

Or maybe it was started and never finished.

Either way, much of the biggest excuses people tell themselves, are the ones related to time.

Before any tasks, goals or personal changes are acted upon, the mind automatically measures out the time it will require to accomplish or complete these things.

Let's take a quick look back at history.

In the late 18th century, Robert Owens started a campaign to have people work for no more than 8 hours per day.

His slogan was "eight hours labor, eight hours recreation and eight hours rest."

Ford Motor company supported Owen's message and method implementing it into their business model in 1914.

The popularity and acceptance of this method was soon followed by many other industries and the rest was history.

Speaking of history, it's worth mentioning that the Ancient Babylonians, were credited for the hour being made up of 60 minutes.

So, I'm sure you are asking, what does this have to do with anything?

Chapter 6: TIME

Well, breaking it down in the simplest form, the amount of time you are programmed to follow in a day is actually man made.

Therefore, at any given moment, you have the ability and the right to create your own time blocks to live by.

When you truly want to accomplish something that requires you to add it into your daily schedule, you will have to make adjustments.

For example, if you have a desire to get into shape, you're going to have to find the time to exercise.

You may have to wake up earlier or stay up later, either way you have to change your current operating time blocks in order to accomplish the task.

Here are a few people who don't let time, stop their grind!

Jack Dorsey, Twitter Founder and Square CEO, spends an equal amount of time at both businesses during the day which is usually 8 to 10 hrs., at both.

Marissa Mayer, Yahoo CEO, prides herself on working up to 130 hours a week and sleeps 4 hours per night.
She catches up on sleep during week-long vacations every four months

Dallas Mavericks' Owner, Mark Cuban, didn't take a vacation for seven years while starting his first business. He routinely stayed up until 2 am learning about new software.

So, what does this mean to you?

Chapter 6: TIME

Whether you have already taken advantage of the extra hours in a day or you're ready to change how you look at time, it first starts with prioritizing your Time Management.

One of the best ways to begin this process is to first identify and eliminate your distractions.

Distractions are the number one enemy to progress.

"Nobody made a greater mistake than he who did nothing because he could do only a little."
-Edmund Burke

How many times have you pre-scheduled a productive moment that was interrupted during the day, with things that had nothing to do with the goal you were trying to accomplish?

Did the phone ring?

Did a text message come through?

Since the new age of smartphones, there seems to be a hidden mandatory rule for some people, that if the phone rings or someone sends a non-emergency text, you must stop and reply or answer it immediately.

Did that notification from social media draw your attention and now you've spent 15mins responding to posts, comments, or inbox messages?

There again, another hidden rule that it's more interesting to see what Jane is talking about on social media, than it is for you to finish that important email or word document.

Chapter 6: TIME

How about the talkative friend, co-worker or mate who always seems to have the latest news to share right when you were just about to create that masterpiece.

It's true, some of the most distracting elements come in the form of tiny innocent moments.

We're not saying this is you but, if it is, creating a "no call / no answer time frame" will increase your daily productivity. Time itself can also become a distraction.

Having too much open time can cause us to push back, delay and reschedule something productive simply because you've found a "better time" to do it.

For instance, today you were finally going to organize your closet the way you have always dreamed of.

Color coding each section of clothes, matching the pair of shoes, etc.

You placed this date on the calendar a week ago and now the time is finally here.

You began to pull all the things out of the closet and lay them in a pile.

After an hour or two, you decided to take a short break.

The break lasted much longer than you planned because you got distracted by something like we talked about earlier.

Now you return to the pile of things on the floor, took one look at it and immediately began saying.... "*I did a great job today; I can finish the rest tomorrow because I'm home all day.*"

Chapter 6: TIME

So, you spend the rest of this day doing random things rather than finishing what you previously scheduled for today simply because you had more time to do it.

Everyone successful, or not, has the same amount of time in the day.

How you use those spare moments of time, truly depends on you and what you are trying, or not trying to accomplish.

So note, if you ever find yourself saying, you don't have enough time in the day, measure the amount of time you spend doing those distracting things verses the productive things and find those few extra moments you need to accomplish your goals.

-end chapter 6-

Chapter 7:
MOTIVATION
(Making Opportunity The Immediate Vision And Top Initiative Over Necessities)
DeMario's Story

"We must be willing to let go of the life we planned so as to have the life that is waiting for us."
-Joseph Campbell

Chapter 7: MOTIVATION

More than just a great acronym and title, MOTIVATION has life-changing attributes when realized and applied.

To make this chapter more meaningful and real, we'll share a story around how this book's Co-Author, DeMario McIlwain, used motivation to change the trajectory of his career.

Let's go back to the Summer of 2002

Fresh out of the military and ready to jump back into civilian life as he once knew it, lifelong artist and world traveled self-taught musician, DeMario McIlwain, was looking for his next big opportunity.

With slow work and facing the challenges associated with being a transitioning veteran acclimating back into the market, you could only imagine McIlwain's excitement when he was approached to join a recording studio, as a producer and engineer.

The music scene was not new to McIlwain, who'd spent many years of his life sidelining as a producer for multiple independent artists.

Anyone could see that music was truly his God-given talent & passion, which is why he was all too happy to accept the offer.

The big day had finally come, and it was time for McIlwain to meet and impress the owner of the studio, yet there was just one small problem.

When McIlwain arrived, he embarked on a room full of strangers comprised of other hopeful musicians and producers looking for their chance to work with the popular local studio.

Chapter 7: MOTIVATION

It quickly became clear that the owner had personally invited many others to the same opportunity as well, to see who the final candidate for the studio position would be.

This meant contrary to what McIlwain had hoped, there was no exclusive invite for his talents alone.

Instead just an open free for all that required candidates to compete for the seat.

"I've been tricked." McIlwain thought silently to himself.

Just at the moment, the owner took to the front of the room and begin explaining exactly what he was looking for in an ideal candidate; along with his visions for the future.

As McIlwain intently listened on, he couldn't help but to become excited as he learned more about the owner's history.

As the story went, the owner had previously been a singer who replaced Sam Cooke, with the Soul Stirrers.

The owner then concluded by sharing that he, his sons and studio staff, were still very much actively involved in current day music industry affairs.

In fact, he shared how his team had developed, produced or recorded mainstream acts such as Toni Braxton, Groove Theory, The Neptunes, Calvin Richardson and many more.

Armed with this information, McIlwain felt this would be a dream job.

Without shame and in full transparency, the owner continued with the following message, *"Only one of you in this room, will take advantage of this opportunity."*

Chapter 7: MOTIVATION

The owner made it clear that this was not a competition, yet instead a simple test of MOTIVATION to see who wanted the position the most and who would be totally dedicated to the team.

McIlwain understood this and was up for the challenge.

The owner also knew that most people in this industry would jump ship quickly when they found out that the opportunity wouldn't be all about glamour, parties, and money and therefore he had to choose wisely.

Throughout that first day, McIlwain, who didn't know anyone, sat in the back of the room listening and watching.

Many of the candidates seemed to know each other sharing their excitement and expressing how they were going to be in the studio learning the systems and bringing in lots of new business.

Having just relocated back to the area, after being in the U.S. Army for 10 years, with no previous clientele to attract and nothing in common with the others, McIlwain felt the odds stacked against him in every way.

But that wouldn't stop a motivated McIlwain from trying his best to win this opportunity.

Still holding down a basic 9 to 5 job making just enough to pay the bills, McIlwain figured out a way that he could come to the studio after work and stay until he was no longer needed sleeping when he could.

Chapter 7: MOTIVATION

No matter what, he knew he needed to give it all he had and, in the days, to come, McIlwain did exactly that.

Day 2, McIlwain, was ready to execute his plan as he arrived at the studio late in the evening armed with a purpose & with his game face on; he was ready for whatever came his way.

Greeted at the door, McIlwain entered the room and to his surprise, yet again, there were others there but this time far fewer than before.

Committed to keeping his head in the game, McIlwain took copious notes and instructions as he looked forward to the week's remaining tasks.

Day 3 dealt with much of the same routine, but this time even fewer people than day 2.

Noticing a pattern, McIlwain had high hopes of being the last man standing which also became his silent motivation.

Pleased to see his steady determination, this time the owner greeted McIlwain at the door with an invitation to join client studio sessions, *"feel free to watch a session or two, you don't have to stay too long if you have to go."*

Feeling honored, McIlwain smiled and replied with, *"Thank you, Sir."* However, in the back of his mind, he knew he was prepared to stay late, later than the others, even if it took all night.

By midnight, McIlwain finally left the studio for his hour-long drive back home filled with excitement and curious to see who the next day's remaining candidates would be.

Chapter 7: MOTIVATION

"Would there be fewer people than before or possibly even none at all," he wondered.

By Day 4, just like clockwork, McIlwain walked into the studio doors and noticed his prayers had in-fact been answered.
As it turned out, none of the other candidates were there. The owner walked out, looked around and asked a rhetorical question, *"I guess the others had something to do today?"*

McIlwain smiled and thought to himself, *"Yes Sir, I guess so."*

This routine repeated itself over the next few days, as McIlwain would enter the studio and sit by the control room, day after day waiting for his chance.

Careful not to interrupt and out of the way of the studio workers, McIlwain would quietly watch every move the recording engineers made and how they worked with artists recording new music.

On occasion, McIlwain would bring the studio staff drinks and snacks, as he knew they probably hadn't had a break working long days and nights.

Known for its celebrity clientele, one day the guitarist from Reba McIntire's band came into the studio to lay down a few tracks.

In-between tour dates, the guitarist needed to quickly get in and out, yet there was one major problem stopping this plan, the session engineer had been stuck in traffic.

Chapter 7: MOTIVATION

Now worried, the owner noticed McIlwain sitting by the door and asked: *"do you know how to work this equipment?"* He replied quickly with *"Yes, Sir!"* as he jumped in the control seat.

Although nervous and unsure of some of the system's functions, McIlwain took control of the board, just as he had seen the other engineers do.

Within an hour, the music was fully recorded, everyone was happy and smiling and thanking McIlwain for a job well done. The original session engineer, who had eventually made it in sneaking through the back door, gave McIlwain a thumbs up for the work he had done for this client.

Proud and pleasantly surprised, the owner took McIlwain to the side and offered him a key to the building, as well as an opportunity to run [Studio B], with an option to share profits made from this partnership.

Excited and eager to get started, McIlwain saw this as a dream come true moving too quickly accept the position.

The next day, McIlwain was on his way to his day job daydreaming about all he wanted to do at the studio later that night, when he decided to bypass his exit and head straight for the studio.

Why put off later the things we can do now?

At that moment, McIlwain didn't know how this was going to turn out, nor did he know if he would be able to make a living working in this new studio.

All he knew was that this was the opportunity he had always hoped and dreamed of, which is what mattered most.

Chapter 7: MOTIVATION

While this would be the very beginning of McIlwain's first entrepreneurial experience, it certainly would not be the last.

Through this opportunity, McIlwain gained so much confidence, that he not only became a great engineer but went on to advance in other areas owning his own business & never again looking back to a basic 9 to 5.

The true moral of this story is broken down into two parts.

MOTIVATION - Making Opportunity The Immediate Vision and Top Initiative Over Necessities.

Do you think he made this opportunity his immediate vision?

If you said yes, you are correct.

Once McIlwain was presented with an opportunity that aligned with his passion, it got his immediate attention and became all he thought about, to the point of endless pursuit showing up opportunity-ready daily.

In this story, McIlwain sacrificed many elements willing to do without various things for the one thing he believed in.

However, before we conclude this story, it's important to understand how you define success when you're following your purpose.

Many times, success does not equal millions of dollars or world-wide fame in the beginning.

Instead, success might simply be the art of creating a vision and making a living doing what you love!

-end chapter 7-

Chapter 5   MOTIVATION

While this would be the very height of Vedic wisdom, entrepreneurial experience, in reality would never be it.

The idea: the opportunity Arjuna saw clearly convince us that is that only be one a vocation of having, but of more — the enjoyment of game or trying to seek more— having to look to a tasks a and...

The choice is: off it is Arjuna is his... do...

KRISHNA: ... Work a, Cape rightly, therefore and to preserve Arjuna, Jeeva...

It is... a nature this opportunity which the every time is have of...

If you said... at present...

Once McKenna has persevered with a... doubt while enough... his vocation, it is all the for machine is known and no small in western sense is to have in a ... hope that showing in any martially-ready...

In fact every ah... wonder addition to the one in... whatfully, all is... thinks, for that are going to tell...

However, Keena was a a oldnabout this store, if arjuna or Surrender are know you define success style... KURU, the being join a me... e

story time... not as choes how equal in all to is in life... as world... could... force in the beginning...

Instead, success might simply be the art of creating a vision of... at... living doing what you love...

— and enjoying...

78

Chapter 8:
DRIVE
(Determined Resilient Inspiration & Valor for Excellence)
*Dawn Nicole's Story

"Failure will never overtake me if my determination to succeed is strong enough."
-Og Mandino

Chapter 8: DRIVE

DRIVE, more than a catchy acronym and literally what Co-Author, Dawn Nicole, was doing when she got the incredible idea to write her first stage play, DRIVE will always be required when you're looking to start something new.

Let's take a closer look at how Dawn Nicole went from thinking to doing producing & directing her first sold out stage play in a new city, in just under 6 months.

In July 2012, while Dawn Nicole was in route of a five-hour drive, relocating from Richmond, Virginia, to Charlotte, NC., she became inspired to create and produce her very first stage play.

High spirited and creative natured, Dawn Nicole had already written novels, short films and had acted in stage plays her entire life, although she'd never tried her hand at writing an actual full-scale production.

Yet suddenly there she was, immersed with the idea to write, cast and produce her first stage play, for a Spring of 2013 opening date.

Inspired by the hit show, The Office, Dawn Nicole wanted to create a diversified comedic stage play she entitled… *"Thank You For Calling Customer Service!"*

The play would showcase slapstick workplace humor centered around the call center employees paralleled with a deeper more human side that also addressed homelessness and an attempted sexual assault at the office.

Although this grand idea gave Dawn Nicole a renewed sense of hope and excitement, there were just a few challenges she'd have to first face.

Chapter 8: DRIVE

For starters, Dawn Nicole hadn't even touched down yet in her new city, meaning she would need to find steady work in her field, as an IT Business Consultant.

Secondly, she didn't know the Charlotte, NC., art scene and would have to prove herself as a director, new to the area.

Thirdly she'd need to find the time to get the entire project done with limited time. i.e. scripting, casting, directing, rehearsal, marketing and more.

Fourthly, Dawn Nicole would need to find the budget to fund the entire project.

No big deal right? Think again. This, coupled with simultaneously raising a family, buying a home and starting a demanding new career, was described as one of the biggest challenges of Dawn Nicole's adult life.

Yet would you believe she pulled it off?

Not only did Dawn Nicole get it done, but she also did it in record-time, closing on a brand-new home the same day as her stage play's opening night.

A show that would eventually go on to play nine times that year, across the North and South Carolina regions.

A play with sold-out shows that helped her make her mark in a new city proving that the unimaginable was possible with the right amount of DRIVE.

Let's go back to the story to see how Dawn Nicole, a once novice playwright, and director, went from thinking to doing and made a name for herself.

Chapter 8: DRIVE

Having just relocated, it was now August 2012 and Dawn Nicole knew that with a busy schedule, it was important to keep the momentum if she were to pull-off this production without a hitch.

Therefore, she used the power of social media to solicit the interest and support of a regional based co-director and graphic artist.

Having a small team involved, helped Dawn Nicole to stay engaged and made her feel accountable to others to move the project forward.

She calls this step... **Accountability Partners:**

Now that her team was in place, a date was selected, and the team had a time frame to work with.

Establishing a date made it real and actual also giving the graphic artist a date to add on the flyers and promo materials.

She calls this step... **Committing To A Date:**

With a date selected, next up was a venue.

Dawn Nicole realized that paying for a venue first, even before having the cast selected, was a very powerful step since it showed that she meant business and the show was going on regardless.

She felt as if people always needed to know and see that you were showing up to do real business and not just thinking about it. A paid venue in advanced demonstrated this.

She calls this step... **Securing A Venue:**

Chapter 8: DRIVE

Now that the date and venue were secured, the focus was on conserving spending by finding out what resources could be leveraged and repurposed to fit the project's needs.

It was time to begin casting and consequent dress-rehearsals. Since she lived in an apartment at the time, while waiting on her new home to be built, Dawn Nicole got the idea to book her apartment clubhouse, at no charge, for the casting calls and ongoing dress rehearsals.

She calls this step… **Leveraging Resources:**

Things were starting to come together beautifully and Dawn Nicole and her team, couldn't be happier.

The cast had been selected, rehearsals were underway, photoshoots had been scheduled and promo materials were being designed.

By all accounts, things were starting to look up and this project was becoming more real by the day.

Now in early February 2013, with an opening night of April 13th quickly approaching, it was important that Dawn Nicole kept the actors motivated and excited about their involvement.

She did this by constantly reminding the actors of what was in it for them sharing things like the red carpet marketing event she had planned, the coffee shop meet and greets, the media frenzy that was building and how they had the opportunity to grow with the production as more shows continued to open up.

Dawn Nicole found that by keeping the cast abreast of the public's anticipation of their new stage play, the actors felt more privileged and excited to be apart.

Chapter 8: DRIVE

Essentially, she made them feel like stars in their own right and created a sense of culture and community amongst them.

This not only made them more committed to the project yet transformed them into branding and marketing ambassadors.

She calls this step... **Motivating Her Team:**

Now it was time for the marketing and promotions component, something Dawn Nicole had intentionally prioritized to be last, but certainly not least.

She knew how easy it was for production teams to get caught up in early marketing campaigns while managing through crumbling infrastructure, and she didn't want that to be her team.

Dawn Nicole didn't have the time or budget to get the marketing wrong, therefore instead, she waited until things were rock solid before driving heavy media buzz.

Using a big bang effect, she went for radio, digital marketing, meet and greets, red carpet events sponsored by fancy restaurants and outsourced a team to do the heavy lifting.

Her marketing strategy involved excited actors, sponsors, partners, bloggers, magazines and heavy engagement through the play's fan page.

All in all, her strategy paid off with an opening night that broke box office records and turned last-minute patrons away.

She calls this step... **Prioritizing & Delegating Tasks:**

Her cast rocked it and afterward, presented her with flowers and gifts and it was a night to remember.

Chapter 8: DRIVE

Beyond that Spring opening night, her play would go on to run again in the Summer, at Fort Mill Playhouse and finalize with several Dinner Theater style shows in the Fall, running a total of nine times that year. Dawn Nicole recalls being forever grateful that she was able to DRIVE this idea from thinking to doing by not over obsessing and instead, getting out of her head and onto her purpose.

-end chapter 8-

Chapter 9:
LEVERAGE
(Learning Every Valuable & Eligible Resource Available for Greater Expansion)
The BrandDisco© Story

> "It is always your next move."
> -Napoleon Hill

Chapter 9: LEVERAGE

As co-founders of an online development tools company known as BrandDisco©, who works with some of the nation's biggest organizations, we're often asked how we created the company.

We find ourselves constantly explaining that our business began by trying to solve one simple problem.

However, what caused our business to grow was the power of leverage when we had limited resources.

In this chapter, perfect for established or emerging business owners, we'll walk you through how we used the power of leverage to move the needle and provide 5-Winning tips on how you can do the same.

Let's review what happened.

The Problem- In 2016, we were known as a CouplePrenuer team, who was running a Branding and Marketing Company, at the time known as GrowGetter Digital.

There we found ourselves spending lots of upfront time helping entrepreneurs discover their unique value propositions, secret sauce and what made them stand out from their competition.

Like many business professionals, our clients struggled to describe their key differentiators, which made it difficult to market them to ideal potential prospects.

The Idea- As a result, this posed a question that would spark a new idea... "What if we could create itemized personal brand categories to help streamline our client's upfront discovery experience?"

Chapter 9: LEVERAGE

We figured this would help speed up the initial process, provide early and often insights & move our clients to the development stage 50% faster.

The Solution- While we weren't exactly sure of what the solution would look like, we knew it needed to be automated, accurate and able to provide us with valuable data on demand.

The Work & Sacrifice: Armed with a new-found pensive motivation, we spent every waking moment between January and March 2017 whiteboarding and developing a new personal brand technology that we initially believed would be an inhouse proprietary solution.

Because we still depended on our business to survive and didn't have the luxury of venture capital or a large team, we believed we had a short window of time to create, develop and launch our new idea.

This sacrifice meant early mornings, late nights, working through weekends, no extra spending, nor frivolous meetings.

To paint the picture more clearly, let's just say Valentine's Day was spent with us running out to a local bistro to grab a glass of wine and share a dinner plate, an hour before the restaurant closed.

The Proto-Type- After three months of sacrifice and hard work, we finally had a demonstrable prototype.

Looking back, we admit, the earlier version of our solution was quite hideous and archaic, requiring clients to answer 10 free-form text questions before auto computing the final categories themselves.

Chapter 9: LEVERAGE

Although we'd designed, what we thought were extremely marketing savvy questions strategically positioned to evoke thought, we hadn't quite figured out the functionality.

We laugh now, but the reality is, we pulled together and got it done. We weren't intimidated by what we didn't know, instead, instead we were propelled by purpose and what we believed it could be and do.

The Implementation: Over the next few weeks and months, we'd begin to introduce the prototype of our new concept into our work process calling it the "What Your Secret Sauce Tool" and mandating it be done by our new clients as a first step, before an initial meeting.

To gain honest feedback, we also created an auto survey that would go out to users after they'd taken the tool. Through this, we were able to collect candid feedback that led to a seamless redesign and swift improvements.

What was really interesting about this implementation period, is that while the "What Your Secret Sauce Tool" was not exactly user-friendly, no one really pushed back or called it an ugly baby.

Instead, they were all too happy to oblige and wanted to have their peers and partners take it as well.

This demonstrated the potential for our new product to have somewhat of a viral effect, which is something every development team wants to see.

Trial and Error- By September 2017, we had managed to drum up some early local press and were being booked to speak at professional events across the nation.

Chapter 9: LEVERAGE

During this time, our team also figured out how to shorten the "What Your Secret Sauce Tool" down to 8 questions, fully automate its functionality and transform it into a majority multiple choice online assessment.

While archaic, it turned out that the earlier version of our tool, enabled us to collect enough data to create market industry trends and professional character traits needed to advance quickly.

While it would seem, our vision was beginning to unfold right before our very eyes, customers were happier & work was more efficient than ever, there were a few things we didn't see coming such as:

      a. Clients who wanted to license our tools to use with their own clientele
      b. Various industry peers who wanted to be affiliate partners
      c. Learning curves with incorporating our new product into our servicing model

The Work- With all things considered, we realized we needed to think bigger and investigate how to launch our product into the commercial sector.

We changed the name from the "What Your Secret Sauce Tool" to the BrandDisco© Assessment, (short for Brand Discovery), enrolled the help of a pilot team to use our product as account holders and worked to create competitive pricing models.

Chapter 9: LEVERAGE

During this awakening of new-found potential, we also attempted to raise capital where after multiple attempts of being turned down, due to having made no money as of yet and being offered one deal that fell through, we enrolled in a series of pitch competitions and incubator cohorts.

The Launch- By January 2018, after working tirelessly to build, polish and improve the BrandDisco© Assessment, we were ready to introduce our new product to the world.

However, although it solved a real problem, we still needed to quickly determine which group it solved the biggest global problem for.

With this in mind, one of the first things we did was examine which socially relevant causes the BrandDisco© assessment could help solve.

It turned out; we didn't have to look far since the answer was staring us right in the face.

As a company whose Co-founder, DeMario McIlwain, was an Army Veteran, knew all too well how Transitioning Veterans faced challenges marketing themselves and acclimating in a civilian workforce.

Considering that BrandDisco© was originally designed for professionals struggling to describe their key differentiators, we saw this as a win-win solution for the veterans themselves as well as for the Military Transition Leaders who support them.

Understanding this problem and the solution we could bring; our launch strategy was to focus on meeting the needs of the transitioning veteran market.

Chapter 9: LEVERAGE

We launched and officially established BrandDisco© in February 2018 and proudly begin supporting national military transition programs with organizations like Operation Good Jobs by Goodwill, Virginia Department of Veteran Services, Texas Veterans Commission, Onward to Opportunity and more!

Today BrandDisco© has evolved to a full-scale online development tools company helping leaders in various markets to discover, develop and market their people's top talents in less time.

Through trial and error, we discovered who was and who we weren't.

We also realized the difference between the things our tools were capable of vs. the things our tools were really great for.

Evolution...

Today BrandDisco© has evolved to a full-scale online development tools company helping leaders in various markets to discover, develop and market their people's top talents in less time. Through trial and error, we discovered who was and who we weren't. We realized the difference between the things our tools were simply capable of vs. the things our tools were really great for.

Chapter 9: LEVERAGE

See Our Top 5 Tips More Moving Your New Idea To The Next Level:

1. **Be Willing To Go Back To The Drawing Board.** *Especially as you learn more and acquire new talent. Don't get married to your first draft.*
2. **Remember Your Why.** *Why you got started is the same reason why you're still here. Your why will never change. The market, mission, and motto might change but the why remains steadfast. Your why is your purpose.*
3. **Follow The What & The How Will Come.** *Many people start figuring out how before they figure out what. Don't worry about how. Focus on what and the steps for how will appear. Your what is your vision.*
4. **Shut Off The Noise.** *Focus is one of the most under-rated skills. When armed with a purpose, vision, and mission, it's critical to shut off all distractions, pre-select the right people at the table and stay close to the campfire. The place where the magic is happening. Any outside interference can easily cost you weeks or months of setbacks.*
5. **Done Is Better Than Perfect.** *We now live in a society where the winner is the one who makes it happen first. Imperfect or not. Consumers want early access and the opportunity to be early adaptors. The 21st-century buying experience has evolved to where consumers want to feel personally vested as contributors. They are more forgiving than ever before and will eagerly await the multiple iterations or product versions to come. So, let's go from dreaming to doing!*

-end chapter 9-

Chapter 10:
Success Stories From Everyday People

"Success only comes to those who dare to attempt."
-Mallika Tripathi

Chapter 10: Success Stories

Throughout this book, we've taken the time to meticulously layout the many reasons people don't experience faster success, along with real stories of those who've struggled and the detailed steps they've taken to overcome these obstacles.

Now it's time to highlight a few success stories from everyday people who had a vision and the tenacity to move the needle.

We'll begin with Mr. Clarence McIlwain, our beloved father and lifelong entrepreneur; now in his late sixties.

In early 2016, Mr. McIlwain had a vision to host a Celebration of Life Event for the holidays as a way to celebrate Senior Citizens while they were still alive to smell the roses.

Within months of sharing his idea with us, there we were along with so many others, attending his holiday event.

This lavish event, equipped with a photographer, catered food, decorations, a live band, gift giveaways, holiday bliss and so much more, ended up being a smash hit.

His ability to execute with minimal barriers and little stress intrigued us, as we wondered how someone could easily go from dreaming to doing and pull-it-off in excellence.

More importantly, we wanted to know what made him move the needle, while many of our very own highly tenacious driven clients had ideas dating back to the late 1990's, that were still sitting somewhere in a scrapbook. Unexecuted, unrequited & unsung great ideas.

This notion forced us to take a closer look at the steps Mr. McIlwain had taken to get out of his head and onto his purpose.

Chapter 10: Success Stories

"I've learned to always seek God first in everything I do. It always works out best for me."
– Clarence McIlwain, CEO of Mr. Mac's Lawn Service.

The Celebration of Life:

In early 2016, Mr. Clarence McIlwain shared how he was filled with a vision to host a celebration of life event - only this wouldn't be any ordinary event.

Instead, this would be for senior citizens who were in their golden years, married, settled-down and excited about life. Mr. McIlwain's vision was to host a fun-filled glorious event that celebrated seniors, almost as a tribute to them.

He envisioned this as an annual event and an opportunity to create unforgettable memories.

At first thought, the idea while admirable, sounded like some big feat to pull off; and you must understand that Mr. McIlwain was no world-class celebrity event planner with tons of cash and global resources.

Yet rather a God-fearing servant leader and owner of a landscaping company who was filled with a vision.
This is why when he mentioned his vision to us and asked that we somehow be involved, we graciously accepted the opportunity.

Quite frankly, as the Branding and Marketing Strategists we were at that time, we were thinking…

"Of course, he's going to need our help planning, marketing, finding resources and so much more."

Chapter 10: Success Stories

Right? Wrong!

Instead, life happened, and Mr. McIlwain moved the needle without waiting around on us.

Though we meant well, we became extremely busy with our own agendas and inadvertently dropped the ball.

Looking back, we now realize just how bad that sounds.

However, summer turned to fall, fall turned to winter and before we could blink, we went from being introduced to Mr. McIlwain's big idea, to being invited as attendees.

We can only imagine that in the absence of our help, Mr. McIlwain's determination to move the needle, along with the support of his loving wife and our mother, Margaret McIlwain, he became committed to getting this done.

Just a few weeks before the event, with the hardest work already done, we received a call to add a few final touches to the flyer.

"You're Invited to The Celebration of Life Event..."

Were the headlining words Mr. McIlwain requested us to add. To say the least, we were totally blown away.

"What about all of the event planning?" We wondered.

We learned it had already been done.

Through support and taking it one step at a time, Mr. McIlwain was able to get it planned.

Chapter 10: Success Stories

"What about the venue, the food, the music, the tickets, the marketing?" We thought to ourselves, feverishly trying to make sense of it all.

We discovered this had already been done as well.

Through asking around and the help of trusted friends, Mr. McIlwain had secured a venue, organized a caterer, booked a band, pre-sold tickets and collected money, all before having the final flyer.

At this point, we were simply stunned and amazed. Impressed by his persistence, we completed the flyer and looked forward to his upcoming event.

The big day finally came only to see that **The Celebration of Life Event** was a pure success, just as he envisioned.

Through his actions, Mr. McIlwain taught us an extremely powerful lesson, a vision fueled by faith, is the only ammunition you need to get started.

In absence of a fancy plan, one-hundred hours of planning, or an army of ten thousand troops, a vision starts with the first step and baby-steps, are still steps.

It's all a matter of perspective.

If you overthink it, it will become harder than it should be.

As we like to say, complication is the over analyzation of simplicity.

Instead, if you focus on what you want *(the vision)*, then the how *(the strategy)*, will come.

Chapter 10: Success Stories

We've learned, sometimes you must take the first step in order to see the next step.

Thank you, Mr. McIlwain, for your valuable lessons!

MyPowerMom.com

Let's take a closer look at Ayanna Edwards.

Wednesday, January 10, 2018, a woman walked into a swank coffee shop with a notebook full of ideas, concepts and thoughts, which had been previously buried and tucked-away.

That woman was Ayanna Edwards, and she was there to meet with us – an excited client who was suddenly ignited with a newfound flame and an unrelenting sense that 2018 was going to be her breakthrough year!

The year that something epic would happen.

The year her ideas would break free from their life-sentences and become living, breathing manifestations of dreams no longer deferred.

The year she would finally get out of her head and onto her purpose by going from thinking to doing and we could not have been more honored to have been the team to support her worthy cause.

So, there we sat, nestled quaintly across each other in a bright corner with nothing more than the sounds of social chatter, a roaring fireplace, two cups of coffee - lightly blended and the unanswered question which loomed over our heads like a cumulus cloud.

Chapter 10: Success Stories

"*What vision were we there to build?*"

Edwards began by intently sharing how she had all of these unfinished ideas that had never transpired beyond their original pages.

Regardless of her reasons why, albeit fear, doubt, trust, lack of capacity or something more, she refused to enter another year repeating this same cycle.

Needless to say, we went to work right away, envisioning, crafting and building what her concept would be.

Edwards landed on an amazing idea to build an online community of driven working moms who could share, learn and contribute strategies toward motherhood.

We went through rounds of design, development, and strategy even changing the launch date a few times until we finally had a simple solid plan.

One that entailed a current state launch with visions for a future state.

Meaning, we agreed to launch a scaled-down version of the master plan to gain interest and excitement.

By October 2018, Edwards had a successful grand launch of her MyPowerMom.com business pitching to a packed room of working moms.

The event was perfectly equipped with sweet treats, fashion, jewelry, information, and her new MyPowerMom.com Quiz!

Chapter 10: Success Stories

It took Edwards, motivation, and determination to see this outcome and more importantly, it took her to simply get started by going from thinking to doing.

Overcoming Against All Odds: The Jaysen T. Crump Story

"My success is not measured by how much money I make, it's measured by the fact that every day I do what I love, for myself. I'm happy I can make a living for my kids and provide work for others."
-Jaysen T. Crump, CEO of Special EFX Pressure Washing LLC

Jaysen T. Crump is the proud owner of Special EFX Pressure Washing LLC, a Florida based company established in 2008, which focuses on commercial and residential pressure washing and painting.

Today Special EFX Pressure Washing, is a multi-team operation which proudly employs work crews and provides a great lifestyle for Crump and his family.

However, what many people don't know is that, as a young man coming up, Crump, had a rough start.

As a young father in the early 90's, Crump, didn't get the chance to finish high school as planned, instead life had a different path for him.

Desperate to make ends meet for his new family, Crump found himself going from job to job determined to make a way. Night jobs, morning work, part time gigs and temporary labor, nothing seemed to fit the bill.

Chapter 10: Success Stories

Between sharing one car, managing the demands of a premature newborn - with another on the way, and sheer lack of sleep, Crump's situation was not ideal for a young man trying his best to thrive.

Often times, he found himself frustrated and stressed out feeling as if he could see a better life, that he just couldn't reach.

Although he eventually managed to get his GED and later a welding certificate, with limited resources, no handouts and running out of options, Crump even resorted to street hustling to survive.

Now for some people, these circumstances would have been enough to permanently give up, or give in. Give-up on their hopes and dreams or give-in to a life of quick hustles and easy money.

But Crump was determined to be different, still young, hopeful and ambitious, he refused to let his circumstances at the time, define who he would become.

Motivated to take control of his own destiny, create a platform for his children and make enough money for an honest living, Crump decided it was time for a change.

Armed with a newfound vision, Crump was going to start a pressure washing business. One that allowed him to begin pressure washing whatever he could to get paid - building relationships and learning more along the way.

Having been raised in a family where he watched his mother, Natalie Crump, work hard for everything and instill the same in her children, Crump had been no stranger to hard work.

Chapter 10: Success Stories

After all, this was the same guy who at age 14 shoveled snow for money during bitter cold New England winters to pay for things we wanted, and Crump still had that same work ethic buried within.

Today Crump has been in business for over eleven years and may not ever describe himself to others as an overcomer since he doesn't see himself as a walking success story.

But we do, which is why we asked permission to highlight him in this book.

Inspired by those who take the first step to go after their dreams, Crump, a Business Owner, family man and our brother, is an example of getting out of your head and onto your purpose.

Jaysen T. Crump reminds us that rather than focusing on what we don't have, we can take the best of who we are, and overcome anything against all odds!

-end chapter 10-

Chapter 11:
Twenty-Nine Winning Tips & Actionable Strategies With Simple Exercises

Chapter 11: Twenty-Nine Winning Tips & Actionable Strategies With Simple Exercises

At this point, congratulations are definitely in order, as you've almost read this entire book and perhaps have been inspired to take action along the way.

If this is the case, then we've accomplished exactly what we were setting out to do by motivating you to move the needle.

Although this book was designed to provoke thought that leads to change, we know that change won't come without action - and action is ignited by vision!

Therefore, as a bonus gift to you, we've taken the time to outline twenty-nine winning tips below, broken down by chapter along with a 6-Step Vision & Action Plan Kick Starter.

So, let's outline a few next steps:

Step 1: Start by reviewing the quick reference tips below to determine which area resonates with you the most. *Maybe it's all or just a few.*

Step 2: From there, feel free to circle, or take notes of the tips in each respective section defining how you can make them meaningful to you.

Chapter 11: Twenty-Nine Winning Tips & Actionable Strategies With Simple Exercises

Chapter 1: TRUST TIPS - Taking Risks Under Suppose Threat

1. Trust your gut - you know more than you know!
2. Leave room for the magic and watch the possibilities unfold!
3. Get to know the real you - the authentic self can outwit, outsmart and outlast, the manufactured self any day.

Chapter 2: FEAR TIPS - Failure of Each Action & Result

4. Do it afraid – bravery is not the absence of fear but the presence of faith!
5. You owe it to yourself to try – one step in the right direction is worth more than 1,000 years of thinking about it.
6. Let your fear foster something fierce!

Chapter 3: PERFECT TIPS - Perceived Expectations Restricting Forward, Execution, Completion & Tasks

7. Done is better than perfect- therefore give the world the best you have and be willing to make it better as you evolve.
8. It doesn't need to be perfect; it just needs to be available!
9. Start with what's necessary - perfection is the enemy of progress!

Chapter 11: Twenty-Nine Winning Tips & Actionable Strategies With Simple Exercises

Chapter 4: DOUBT TIPS - Debating Over Uncertainties Before Trying

10. Don't let where you are today doubt who you can become tomorrow.
11. It takes pure bravery to step out of what's already known, into the darkness of what's yet to be discovered.
12. Beware of other's doubt - if you buy someone else's opinion of you, then you must also buy their lifestyle.

Chapter 5: TRUTH TIPS - Time Reveals Unique Talents & Habits

13. No one can speak your truth but you, therefore take the time to define your truth & why it matters to you.
14. Truth begins by admitting, where you are today is not where you desire to be tomorrow.
15. Don't be afraid to reintroduce your new truth- those who once KNEW you, need to know the NEW you!

Chapter 6: TIME TIPS - The Initial Mental Entrapment

16. We all have the same amount of time, just not the same amount of responsibilities, therefore spend your time wisely.

17. When spending time with other driven people, spend time with people who have the same amount to risk as you.
18. You must show up, no matter how long it takes you - what happened before you came doesn't matter if you don't show up to tell your story!

Chapter 11: Twenty-Nine Winning Tips & Actionable Strategies With Simple Exercises

Chapter 7: MOTIVATION TIPS - Making Opportunity The Immediate Vision And Top Initiative Over Necessities

19. Determination & commitment to your vision will help you remain motivated when you want to quit.
20. Motivation is not about your dedication when it's easy, it's about your dedication when it's hard.
21. Motives are not made equal - know what motivates you. People are motivated by different things (i.e. money, fame, success, peace, happiness, health, wealth, etc.)

Chapter 8: DRIVE TIPS - Determined Resilient Inspiration & Valor for Excellence

22. Drive is about creating a circle, climate and culture that fuels your success.
23. Some primary factors to fueling your success are obtaining accountability partners, commitment to a goal, securitization of things needed, leveraging of resources, motivating a team, prioritization and delegation of tasks.
24. Without DRIVE nothing moves.

Chapter 9: LEVERAGE TIPS - Learning Every Valuable & Eligible Resource Available for Greater Expansion

25. Be willing to go back to the drawing board, especially as you learn more and acquire new talent.
26. Remember your why, as why you got started is the same reason why you're still here.
27. Follow the what & the how will come.
28. Shut off the noise, focus is one of the most under-rated skills.
29. People are more dedicated when they feel personally vested - allow for this type of collaborative growth.

This concludes our 29 winning tips. For clarity & support go to @ OntoYourPurpose.com to learn how to apply each tip to your purpose. Our team can't wait to hear from you!

Step 3: Now that you've assessed and reviewed the above tips, feel free to use this 6-Step Vision & Action Kick Starter to begin mapping out your plan.

Free feel to answer these questions on a separate sheet of paper.

6-STEP VISION & ACTION PLAN KICK-STARTER

Instructions: Complete the 6-Step worksheet numbered from left to right responding to the *inquisitive prompts* within each step designed to provoke thought & perspective.

Define Your Vision
In the next 12-Months

1. Who do you want to BE?

   Why is this important to you?

2. What do you want to DO?

   Why is this important to you?

3. What do you want to HAVE?

   Why is this important to you?

Set A Simple Action Plan
In the next 6-Months

4. Who do you need to KNOW or get introduced to first to support your vision?

   What do you need from them?

   What's in it for them?

5. What do you need to GET to support your vision?

   Why is it important that you get this now?

   Once you get this what's next?

6. What next 3-steps do you need to TAKE to support your vision?

   Step 1

   Step 2

   Step 3

All Rights Reserved© BrandDisco© LLC

This concludes the 6-Step Vision & Action Plan Kick Starter. For clarity & support go to @ OntoYourPurpose.com to learn how to apply this plan to your purpose. Our team can't wait to hear from you!

Chapter 11: Twenty-Nine Winning Tips & Actionable Strategies With Simple Exercises

#1: Fun Games and Easy Exercises
From
Chapter 1: TRUST – The Bean Bag Improv Game

A great exercise for building up trust & gut instincts as a group, is an original game we created called Bean Bag Improv by BrandDisco©

Fun and exciting, it works best with 3 or more people in the same group setting and is designed to prove that we know more than we think.

Bean Bag Improv is a great way to help teams and leaders combine and strengthen their impulse with their knowledge base.

Unscripted and unrehearsed, Bean Bag Improv is sure to garner some great laughs and memorable moments.

Try to Avoid politics & religion and think more about People, Places and Things!

Here's how it works:

Improv Leader: Select an Improv Leader who, with bean bag in hand, will start off and oversee the game by choosing random topics before blurting them out as they throw the bean bag to unsuspecting participants.

Note: *Some leaders may take a few moments in advance to write down various topics that should remain a mystery to the unsuspecting participants. There are no time topic or time restrictions and the winner is the person who proves to be the most confident about the random topics while under pressure.*

Chapter 11: Twenty-Nine Winning Tips & Actionable Strategies With Simple Exercises

Person 1: The first unsuspecting participant who catches the bean bag must take 10-15 seconds divulging everything they know related to the Improv Leader's random topic until the Improv Leader yells "Next" _____ followed by the next random topic. (i.e. "Next Brown Spiders.") When person 1 hears next _____ and the Improv Leader's new topic, they immediate throw the bean bag to person 2.

Person 2: The second unsuspecting participant who catches the bean bag from person 1, must take 10-15 seconds divulging everything they know related to the Improv Leader's random topic until the Improv Leader yells "Next" _____ followed by the next random topic. (i.e. "Next Brown Spiders.") When person 2 hears next _____ and the Improv Leader's new topic, they immediate throw the bean bag to any unsuspecting next person. If there were only 2 players, then it would go back and forth between person 1 and 2.

Person 3: The third unsuspecting participant who catches the bean bag from person 2, must take 10-15 seconds divulging everything they know related to the Improv Leader's random topic until the Improv Leader yells "Next" _____ followed by the next random topic. (i.e. "Next Brown Spiders.") When person 3 hears next _____ and the Improv Leader's new topic, they immediate throw the bean bag to any unsuspecting next person.

Chapter 11: Twenty-Nine Winning Tips & Actionable Strategies With Simple Exercises

#2: Fun Games and Easy Exercises

From Chapter 2: FEAR– The Discover Your Passion Exercise

Instructions: If you're on a quest to discover your true passion, answering these 4-questions will help.

Let's Begin:

1. Do you love what you currently do for a living?
_____
_____

2. Do you think & talk about it all the time?
_____
_____

3. Do you get self-satisfaction from it?
_____
_____

4. Would you do it for free if all your needs were met?
_____
_____

Chapter 11: Twenty-Nine Winning Tips & Actionable Strategies With Simple Exercises

Results Key:

-If you have more yes's than no's, you are well on your way to your passion!
-If you have more no's than yes's, then it's time to act and our 6-Step Vision & Action Kick Starter is designed to help you do exactly that.

This concludes our 2-fun exercises. For clarity & support go to @ OntoYourPurpose.com to learn how to apply these to your purpose. Our team can't wait to hear from you!

-end chapter 11

About The Authors

About DeMario and Dawn Nicole McIlwain

Branding & Marketing Teachers, Speakers and Authors, DeMario and Dawn Nicole McIlwain, are family focused and often regarded as a power couple with a purpose.

Husband and Wife Co-founders of a company called BrandDisco©, an Online Development Tools firm headquartered in Fort Mill, South Carolina, The McIlwain's are known as Personal Branding Pioneers for bringing personal branding marketing tools to the corporate arena with the introduction of their Instant Personal Brand Discovery Technology in 2017.

Diverse in every sense of the word, Demario McIlwain, was born in raised in Lancaster, South Carolina while, Dawn Nicole, is from Springfield, Massachusetts adding a dynamic perspective to their harmonious outlook on life and purpose.

Albeit from different cultural upbringings, this coupleprenuer team stems equally from deeply artistic & creative backgrounds with a vast musical and theatrical portfolio that rivals their business accomplishments.

The McIlwain's, who managed to transform their branding & marketing business into a leading signature development tools platform, are passionate about supporting social causes & inspiring others to reach their greatest potential.

As a result, today they enjoy speaking, teaching & motivating the masses to move the needle through their highly anticipated & critically acclaimed new book, Get Out Of Your Head And Onto Your Purpose!

Special Acknowledgments

Our Special Acknowledgments

Writing this book has jogged a remarkable journey of memories, lessons learned and insights that have reminded us of the importance of simply getting started.

In doing so, there were so many great people who inspired certain key-points and chapters that we'd be remiss if we didn't dedicate a section to honor and acknowledge them.

Therefore, we'd like to share Our Special Acknowledgements to:

-Our supportive children, from oldest to youngest, Kenyon, Kamari, Korey, Zahria and Marcquelle, for always showing us that you can get Out Of Your Head And Onto Your Purpose at any age.

-Our loving parents, Mr. Clarence and Mrs. Margaret McIlwain, Mr. Ivan & Patricia Irving and Ms. Natalie Crump, for being a foundational pillar in our early lives. Their unyielding belief that we could do anything has helped us to shape a rewarding sense of resilience.

-People who kept us going with their warm words of encouragement: Keithan McIlwain, Arch-Bishop Anthony Jones, Bess Hurr, Theodore & Pat Parker and Walter Webb.

-Our extended family, team, friends, clients, and supporters for believing and rallying around our visions, successes and this particular book project.

Most importantly, we want to thank you, as a reader of this book.

We wrote this book for you, with the deepest of intentions in hopes that it would truly help to transform your belief system past your inhibitions.

As co-authors, we were careful not to rush or short-change our greatest truths with this book. Instead our hopes were to provide you with meaningful heartfelt content to move you past thinking and onto doing. It is with great joy that we gift this book to you!

www.ingramcontent.com/pod-product-compliance
Lightning Source LLC
Chambersburg PA
CBHW070502100426
42743CB00010B/1730